Are You in THE WILL?

Cynthia J. Eckert Saarie

The opinions expressed in this manuscript are solely the opinions of the author and do not represent the opinions or thoughts of the publisher. The author has represented and warranted full ownership and/or legal right to publish all the materials in this book.

Are You in the Will?
All Rights Reserved.
Copyright © 2014 Cynthia J. Eckert Saarie
v5.0 r1.0

Cover Photo © 2014 JupiterImages Corporation. All rights reserved - used with permission.

This book may not be reproduced, transmitted, or stored in whole or in part by any means, including graphic, electronic, or mechanical without the express written consent of the publisher except in the case of brief quotations embodied in critical articles and reviews.

Forevermore

ISBN: 978-1-4327-9992-2

PRINTED IN THE UNITED STATES OF AMERICA

(This book is set up with LOTS of blank parts on each page for the owner to write notes to themselves. It's Your Book, Mark it up!)

Insanity is the result of doing the same thing over and over again, expecting different results.
— Albert Einstein

Are you tired of the insanity of trying to get right with God and not having any success? Are you trying anything different, or are you just continuing to plug along doing the same thing and wondering why nothing is getting any better? Maybe I can help you with this book.

Pretend for an example that I am driving an Audi R8 5.2. I am cruising along when I discover that I am low on fuel, which happens often because I only get about 13 MPG's in this fast, sleek sports car!

Insanity would suggest that I could just keep driving and not worry about running out of fuel, or I could stop at a gas station and top off my tank.

Our Bible is 66 books of fuel for our lives. It's a filling station that we should stop at frequently if we want to change our lives. I am believing that you are reading this book because you want to make some serious changes in your life. You are tired of the insanity. You want to make some changes and are not sure where to begin....

So let's start at the Beginning…

In the beginning there is God. God made the Heavens and the Earth. God Said, **"Let there be light."** and there was light. God Said, **"Let there be an expanse between the waters, separating water from water."** God Said, **"Let us make man in Our image."** Get the message, GOD SAID. Nothing has ever been made by God without "God Said." **Genesis 1:3-26**

Here's a hint, in order for us to start making changes, we must Speak the Words of God. Reading those words is NOT good enough, We Must Speak Them. Those words of God are printed in His Holy Bible. We were made in God's Image. God is Spirit, we, are also a piece of God's Spirit, housed in a body. We posses a Soul, or a Will of our own. We can make our own decisions, we decide who we are. When we read God's Will in His Bible, we align our minds with the Will of God. God has a plan for your life. He knew you before you were a gleam in your parent's eye. He had a plan all laid out for you and your perfect life, long before you were born.

By reading the Bible we are learning how to find out what that Will of God is for our lives. We can choose to mold our lives to God's Plan for our life, or we can listen to the words of the devil, the words of the world. Learning how and making ourselves Speak God's Words is the first place to start. We have always and always will have a choice on who's words we listen to and act upon. Chose Wisely!

The Holy Bible is a book of Covenants, or Promises that God has made to the People of God. It's God's Will, the Old and the New Testaments. When someone dies, the Last Will and Testament is read to the people who inherit the property. In these Promises God said He Wills to take care of us, protect us, heal and restore us, make us prosperous and whole, nothing missing and nothing broken in every area of our lives. Blessed. We need to find out if YOU ARE IN THE WILL?

What must the People of God do to become Blessed? First and foremost you must Profess: Speak with your Mouth that you Believe in God the Father, the Son, Jesus, and the Holy Spirit. Confess with your MOUTH, that Jesus is your Lord and Savior. This is a Faith statement that we speak out loud, and doing that will make everything else fall into place.

Say this statement, over and over, and over and over, until you Believe what you speak.

I believe that Jesus Christ is my Lord and Savior. Jesus, was sent by God the Father, to earth as a baby, born to the Virgin Mary, as prophesized in the Old Testament, to grow up and walk and live with us as a man. He lived a sinless life and died on a cross to take onto himself our sins, and to fulfill the Covenants of Promise. Jesus exchanged his life for God's promise to give the Covenants of Promise to us, the gentiles. God gave it to us, the ones not originally covered under the laws, because we were not the Jewish children of Israel. God first made the Promise to Abraham and to Jesus, as Abraham's Seed.

Galatians 3:16 Now to Abraham and his seed were the promises made. He does not say, "And to thy seeds", as in many, but to Thy Seed, as in one seed, which is Christ Jesus.

Abraham started the Blessed nation of God, he became the father of many nations and all found favor with God.

Jesus raised Himself again to life, and now lives and interacts with us daily, minute by minute, with the Holy Spirit. And I believe what Jesus did for me, and I am now in Jesus, and I am in the Will. God said it, I believe it! I am now a child of God, and I am also able to claim God's promises.

Why do we have to say this out loud with our mouth? Because when you get something in your heart and mind, it automatically starts coming out of your mouth because it's what you believe. By practicing saying what you believe out of your mouth, you help drive it home into your heart and mind. We go by God's example to Speak His Word. When we speak what we believe, we become what we speak. If we speak health and prosperity, we become healthy and prosperous.

For the thing that I greatly feared is come upon me, and that which I was afraid of is come unto me. Job 3:25

Have you ever known people, or maybe even yourself, who complains that they are broke? Or that they're sick and tired? Or something's always wrong? They are self fulfilling prophecies! They ARE broke, they ARE sick and tired.......

Write here some of Your FORMER complaints...

_____

_____

_____

Now after saying this we can move forward with my mission to teach you about being in God's Will and what you as a child of God are entitled to in This Life **before you die.** We must decide we believe that Jesus is the Son of God, and have faith and believe in Him before we can procede. Without that absolute faith, we come to a complete stop. We must first choose that we believe. If you are at an impass right now, keep reading, I will help you make that leap of faith with the Word of God, our Bible. You really do want to know what's in the Will!

Imagine, first of all, that we must study and learn what God has to say to us by reading, Speaking, meditating and absorbing the lessons in the Bible. Our God has a Will that you inherit the Good News and many wonderful promises that He has put in place to give us a Glorious and Wonderful Life! What a shame it would be if you get all through with your life, struggling and suffering, year after year, when you were in God's Will and had inherited Prosperity, Blessings and Abundance, and never got the memo that you were in the Will? God has many laws for us to follow, but they mostly boil down to the Law of Life, and the Law of Death. Whatever you currently believe, put it aside for awhile so we can go through the Bible and see what it has to say. You can now be smiling because you have been found and now you have the title deed to this Will and you are about to begin your journey towards a blessed life!

And God is able to make all grace, every favor and earthly blessing come to you in abundance, so that you may always and under all circumstances and whatever the need be, self-sufficient, possessing enough to require no aid or support and furnished in abundance for every good work and charitable donation. II Corinthians 9:8.

Why is this so?

For the god of this world has blinded the unbeliever's minds, preventing them from seeing the illuminating light of the Gospel of the glory of Christ, Who is the Image and Likeness of God. II Corinthians 4:4

Remember that you were at that time separated from Christ, utterly estranged and outlawed, and strangers from the Covenants of Promise, having no hope, and without God in this world. Ephesians 2:12

Why did God do this?

For who so ever finds me, finds life and draws forth and obtains favor from God. Proverbs 8:35

We must find God and His Will for our lives. And what are these Covenants of Promise that we should have?

The Lord said to Abram: "Go out from your land, from your relatives, and your father's house to the land that I will show you. I will to make you a great nation, and I will to make your name blessed. And everyone that blesses you, I will to bless them and to those that curse you, I will to curse them. And all the peoples on the earth will be blessed through you." Genesis 12:1-4

Who is Abram and why does God want to make his life so great?

The Lord came to Abram, "Do not be afraid, Abram. I am your sheild: your reward will be very great." Genesis 15:1

But Abram said, "Lord God, what can You give me, since I am childless and the heir to my house is not my son, but Eliezer of Damascus, a slave born in my house?" And God said to Abram, " Eliezer will not be your heir, but a son from your own body will be your heir." And God said, " Look at the sky and count the stars, if you are able to count them. Your offspring will be that numerous." Genesis 15:5

God told Abram that He will make a Covenant of Promise showing that He Will do as He promised. God told Abram to gather a three year old cow, a three year old ram, a three year old female goat, a turtledove and a young pigeon. Split them down the middle and lay the pieces so the blood mingles in the middle, but do not split the birds. Genesis 15:9+10

God then came as a lighted torch and passed through the blood, sealing the promise in blood. Genesis 15:17

In the days of old, people sealed the deals they made with blood. They cut their hands and locked their hands together sealing their deal in blood. These covenants and promises were to last as long as the men lived and ended upon their deaths. **God promised Abram that His Covenant of Promise would last forever.**

Abram was ninety-nine when God promised he would become the father of many nations. His wife, Sarai, was ninety when God told Abram she would be the mother of his son. Abram laughed. God told him that his descendants would outnumber the stars, and the sand by the sea, and still Abram didn't believe God, because he and his wife were so very old.

God then told Abram that He was going to change his name. God changed Abram's name to Abraham, which means "Father of many Nations," and changed his wife, Sarai's name to Sarah, "Mother of many Nations." Genesis 17:5 and 15

For all the land which you see Will I give it to you, and to the Seed, forever.
Genesis 17:9

And God said, "Is anything impossible for the Lord? In about a years time, Sarah will bear a son." Genesis 18:10

For when God made his Covenant of Promise to Abraham, He swore by Himself, since He had no one Greater than Himself whereby to swear by. Saying, Blessing, I certainly Will to bless you and I Will to multiply you. Accordingly God also, in His desire to show more convincingly and beyond doubt to those who were to inherit the Promise, the Unchangeableness of His purpose and plan, confirmed His Promise with an oath. Hebrews 6:13, 14, 17.

This is the Will of God, that the children of God are blessed. Now think on this for a moment. God CAN NOT lie. It's impossible. Why is it impossible for God to lie? Because through Faith, what ever God SAYS actually comes into being. If God said that there is a purple cat in your yard, there would have to be a purple cat in your yard. So when God Swears by Himself that His promises are forever, and that He Wills you to be prosperous and blessed: guess what? You will be prosperous, you will be blessed. **If God promised it somewhere in His Word for someone else, it covers YOU also! That's great news for us all that live in the Will of God!**

Abraham returned to the Valley of the Kings after winning a battle. He met up with King Melchizedek.

Melchizedek, King of Jerusalem, brought out bread and wine: he was the priest of God Most High. And he blessed him and said, Blessed be Abraham by God Most High, Possessor and Maker of Heaven and Earth. And blessed, praised and glorified be God Most High, who has given your foes unto your hand. And Abraham gave him a tenth of all that he had taken from the war. Genesis 14: 17-20.

God is Spirit. Spirit is Pure Energy. God takes the seeds you sow into His Kingdom and converts the energy of that offering into another form. An Exchange of materials. God looks at the purity of your intentions to see where your heart lies. If your heart and intentions line up with the Will of God, He honors your faith and hopes and puts those blessings into your life. Your faith creates the breeding ground for Miracles to appear into your life. Increase your faith, increase your hope, increase the Blessings into your life.

What are some of the things you HOPE for?

_____

_____

_____

And in tradition of Abraham and King Melchizedek, God chooses to give us the Covenants of Promise if we honor Him and do all that is required of us. What is required of us? The laws that lead to Life.

Jesus asked his disciples what are the greatest commandments? What does God expect from us?

Jesus asks us...where is your heart?

F or where your treasure is, there your heart will be also. Matthew 6:21

So where's your heart? What do you spend your time doing and thinking about? Where do you spend your money and resources? What you do and think about is where your heart is. Will God bless someone who doesn't give from their heart? Do you trust Jesus to make an exchange?

These things the Lord hates; a proud look, a lying tongue, hands that shed innocent blood, a heart that manufactures wicked thoughts and plans, feet that are swift to run to evil, and a false witness who breathes out lies. Proverbs 6:16-20.

Can you be trusted? Are you a false believer? Do you profess God, but then your tongue lies? Do you tithe 10% of your pay? Do you go to church every week? Do you pray for your family and friends? Do you offer yourself and your gifts and belongings for others in need to use? Are you considered a Blessing to others? Have you forgiven all those who have done anything against you?

Remember, every good thing comes from God to begin with. Are you so tied up to your things that you won't be able to part with them if that is what is required?

Jesus said unto him, If you wish to be perfect, go and sell all that you have, and give it to the poor, and you shall have treasure in Heaven: and then come, and follow me. But when he heard what Jesus said, he went away very sad, because he had many possessions. Matthew 19:21+22

When the rich young prince asked Jesus what he needed to do to inherit eternal life, he was already rich, he was looking for the eternal Life that Jesus was talking about. The kind of Life that was more fulfilling than the rich life he already had. Jesus told him to sell all of his possessions and give the proceeds to the poor and then follow Him. Jesus knew what the young prince was going to do, He knew the rich prince's heart was not thinking the way God thinks. The young prince went away very saddened. His heart was with his riches. Jesus isn't asking you to give away all of your riches. He is asking you where your heart truly is.... is it tied up in just your money? Your car? Your house? You need to get your priorities to line up with the way God thinks in order to inherit the Eternal Life Jesus is talking about.

Master, which is the Greatest Commandment in the law? Jesus said unto them, You shall love the Lord your God with all your heart, with all your soul, and with all your mind. This is the First and Great Commandment. And the second is like it, You shall love your neighbor as you love yourself. Matthew 22:36-39

I Corinthians 9:10 If you are a sower of hope, you should expect to also partake in the harvest.

You should by faith plead the Blood of Jesus! Christ Jesus shed His Blood to fulfill the blood covenant made with God and Abraham to release the Blessings on this world. A living sacrifice, an exchange, Christ for us. Jesus died taking our sins and cleansing us with His Divine Blood. Now we have access to God's Blessings. We must now willingly and gratefully make an exchange to release this blessing in our lives through our Faith in Jesus. Faith makes it happen.

Are you willing to give a dime of a dollar, of every dollar you make? Are you willing to give of your time, your talents, your energy in exchange for the Blessings from the Covenants of Promise? The people whose heart is only in this world would say no. Sowing a dime of a dollar would not be considered. Think about it. When tax time comes, does your donations for the year add up to a tenth of all you made?

Make a list of some of the things you spend your time and money on, and list some of the places you donate your time and money to.

_____

_____

_____

If you need a job... Do you volunteer your time?

If you need financial help... Do you give of yourself and the things you have to the Glory of God?

If you have a need.... Do you sow a seed into the Kingdom of God?

Harvest can only come if a seed is planted. You are not Giving Away, you are Planting Seeds that Grow!

The blessing of the Lord, it makes truly rich, and adds no sorrow with it.
Proverbs 10:22

What have you Planted? It Will Grow!

_____

_____

_____

Do you have a Grateful heart? Are you grateful for the things you already have in your life and are already grateful for the New Things God is going to put into your life? We expect God to richly bless us. Are you Grateful? And are you Thankful?

Write down some of the things you are Grateful and Thankful for right now. Then, add the New Things you are Grateful and Thankful to God for putting into your life. **We call those things into our life.** List some of them here.

Bless the Lord, O my soul: and all that is within me Bless His Holy Name!
Psalms 103:1

When you give Jesus a place in your life, He will reveal to you the instructions you need to make your life a blessed life, and how to become a blessings to your neighbors. You become blessed to be a blessing. Giving of yourself sets you in line with God's blessings. God would never consider giving a selfish, lying, deceitful person His riches. Loving God first and honoring God's ways, lines you up with how God will bless you and your life.

Be not deceived; God is not mocked: for whatsoever a man soweth, that shall he also reap. Galatians 6:7

You desire and do not have. You murder and covet and cannot obtain. You fight and war. You do not have because you do not ask. You ask and don't receive because you ask with wrong motives, so that you may spend it on your evil desires. James 4:2+3

Knowing that for whatever good anyone does, he will receive his reward from the Lord, whether he is slave or free.
Ephesians 6:8

But my God shall supply all your needs according to his riches in glory by Christ Jesus. Philippians 4:19

Why should you believe that God will hear you and answer your prayers?

And said Jehoshaphat, O Lord, God of our fathers, are You not God in Heaven? And don't You rule over all the kingdoms of the nations? In Your hand are power and might, so that none can stand against You? Didn't You drive out the inhabitants of this land for Your people, Israel, and give it forever to Your friend, Abraham and the descendants of the Seed? They dwelt in it and have built You a sanctuary in it for Your Name, saying, if evil comes upon us, the Sword of judgment, or pestilence, or famine, we will stand before this house and before You, for Your Name is in this house, and cry to You in our affliction and <u>You Will Hear Us and You Will Help Us</u>. II Chronicles 20:6-9

As a Covenant Believer, a child of Abraham, a **Co-Heir with Jesus**: For the measure You deal out will be dealt back to you. God Will Hear Me and My Prayers, and He Will Help. I believe that God hears the prayers and answers the prayers of all covenant people, because HE PROMISED HE WOULD. It's a forever promise to all the heirs of the Covenant. So dream and believe Big. Keep Hope alive. Don't give up. Keep your faith strong. Don't try this for a short period of time and then say you tried God and He didn't do what He promised. You are a work in progress. You may be asking for things you are not ready for yet. Prove ME God, make me aware of what Your Will is for me. Try Me, make me strong in faith so my hopes and dreams are filled. I Know You Hear Me. I am a Covenant Person in your household of faith and You Will to answer my prayers.

Those are encouraging words! Nice to know that God hears me and Wills to answer my prayers, to fulfill all of my hopes and dreams. That God wants me healthy and prosperous. Wow..... I'm feeling better by the minute!

It is the Lord your God that gives you the power to get wealth. Deuteronomy 8:18

The thief (the devil) comes to steal, to kill and destroy. I am come that they may have and enjoy life, and to have it in abundance, till it overflows. John 10:10

So how else do you need to change to get closer and closer into the Will of God for your life? God can't work in the life of an unforgiving heart.

Then Jesus said, "Father, forgive them, because they do not know what they are doing." Luke 23:34

Who do you harbor unforgiveness toward? Who has wronged you to the point that no matter what, you have no plans to EVER forgive them? List them and what the wrong was.

_____

_____

_____

Harboring any unforgiveness is a cancer of the soul. Many people experience such tough and horrible things in their lives, that they feel they could never forgive the person or circumstances they went through. The devil is zeroing right in on that unforgiveness. You have to get rid of it. Hard as it may be, get over it, put it into God's Hands and ask the Lord Jesus to remove the pain and fear the situation brings to you. He Wills you to be whole, Stronger, more capable of all wonderful things and FEAR FREE.

What will Jesus say to you when you die and come before the thrown of God?

Well done thou good and faithful servant! You were faithful over a few things: I will put you in charge of many things. Go Share in your Master's joy! Matthew 25:23

I couldn't think of anything that would bring me more joy, than to hear from Jesus that I was a good and faithful servant of the Most High God! What will keep so many of you that are reading this book from hearing those words spoken about you by Jesus? FEAR. Fear will stop the strongest and bravest person right in their tracks. What will bring on this fear? Doubt. Right back to the doubt that what God has promised won't happen for them. Doubt and fear are the biggest tools of the devil. That evil refers to Lucifer as a "bright morning star" whose rebellion against God caused his fall from the Heavenly Grace that he once lived in.

"How you have fallen from heaven, morning star, son of the dawn! You have been cast down to the earth, you who once laid low the nations! You said in your heart, 'I will ascend to the heavens; I will raise my throne above the stars of God; I will sit enthroned on the mount of assembly, on the utmost heights of Mount Zaphon. I will ascend above the tops of the clouds; I will make myself like the Most High God." Isaiah 14:12-14

Lucifer, the once glorious angel of God decided to exault himself above God. His evil has multiplied to many other evil spirits throughout the centuries. He stalks and searches out any person he thinks he can sway away from God's graces. He plants death and destruction. He brings up any information out of a person's past to make a person not believe God's promises. God says He will bring abundance and health, peace and prosperity. The devil says that just isn't true. And it so easy for us to believe the bad instead of the good. God says you are Blessed! The devil says, "who are you kidding? You've never been anything good, you are stupid to think that you'll ever get anything from God. How can you even think that God cares for you?" So, are you reading these words and thinking the devil's right? We're back at the filling station...

Let him that stole, steal no more: but rather let him labor working with his hands for the things which are good, that he may be able to give to others the things that they need. Ephesians 4:28

But the fearful, and unbelieving, and the abominable, and murders, and whoremongers, and sorcerers, and idolaters, and all liars, shall have their part in the lake which burns with fire and brimstone: which is the second death. Revelations 21:8

The fearful.... those who can't and won't believe God and His word. If you are fearful, then you are also unbelieving. Fear is the devil's playground. He prowls around in your past experiences to find something to bring up from your past to make you doubt that every good thing God has promised you won't happen. He'll try to convince you that God won't prosper you. That you'll die from what ever it is that you are suffering from currently.

He personally bore our sins in His own body on the tree, that we might die to sin, and should live to righteousness. By His wounded stripes (from the whipping and beatings) you are healed. I Peter 2:24

So when you refuse to Believe God, you say you don't believe He died to be a perfect offering in YOUR place. The devil will set up as many roadblocks as he can to trip you up into fearing and doubting God. Just smile. Say to the devil that now you KNOW something Great is about to happen for you, because he is working so hard to keep you down! Believe. Have Faith and speak to those devils that You are the chosen of God and God Wills to Bless YOU! Remember, God created the spirits that haunt, He is greater than all of them! They only have as much power as YOU give them. Don't give them any power. You are the child of the Most High God Almighty! You have no reason to fear.

...for your Father knows what you need before you ask Him. Matthew 6:8

Take therefore no thoughts for tomorrow... Matthew 6:34

You take thoughts. What kinds of thoughts do you entertain in your mind? Do you think on the things of God? Do you spend time in prayer, praying for your family, friends, job, co-workers, President, and especially, for those who hate and persecute you? So with those thoughts you do take, now you speak.

Who do you think about? Who do you pray for, and what do you pray for?

_____

_____

_____

Speak out loud your faith! That by the precious Blood of Jesus, you were redeemed and cleansed from all those old sins. Don't go through the rest of your life doubting the actual existence of God and your part in this world. Believe the promises and know God harkens at the voices of the people who know their covenants. God will hear us and will help us. He has promised to fill our lives with the Glory of the Lord.

What is the Glory of the Lord?

Arise, Shine, for thy light is come, and the Glory of the Lord is risen upon you. Then you shall see and be radiant, and your heart shall thrill and tremble with joy at the glorious deliverance, and be enlarged because the abundant wealth of the Dead Sea shall be turned over to you, unto you shall the nations come with their treasures. Isaiah 60:1+5

Jacob heard Laben's sons complaining, "Jacob has taken away all that was our father's, he has acquired all this wealth and glory from what belonged to our father." Genesis 31:1

Be not afraid when one is made rich, when the wealth and glory of his house are increased: For he dies, he will carry nothing away: his glory will not descend after him. Psalms 49:16+17

Glory is another word for the Blessing, the Anointing. Glory is Spiritual **and** Physical. Non-believers can see the Glory as well as the Believers. It is evident in a person's health, peace of mind, accumulated wealth and complete wellness of a Believer. Covenant people who practice calling out the things they require in their lives, will shine with the Glory of the Lord.

We as Covenant Believers Call Out to God what we require in our lives. It is the Faith that God Hears us that fills the Hope of the items we require. Hope in what God has promised and Faith in God that He Wills to fill that thing we hope for.

Faith is the substance hoped for, the evidence of things not yet seen. Hebrews 11:1

...and calls those things that BE NOT as Though They Were. Who against hope, believed in hope..... Romans 4: 17+18

Faith is the substance, the exchanged material for the materialization of the NEW thing hoped for. How do you acquire Faith? By the Word of the Lord, learning and meditating on the Words of God in His Bible. If your faith needs to be stronger, read more of the Word that leads to Eternal Life. With the Faith you learn, You are the Designer, the Architect, of the Glorious World you live in NOW. You don't have to wait until you die to have the Peace and Beauty and Wonders of Heaven right here on Earth, right now in this lifetime. As we increase our Faith, we start to see those things that we have hoped for and had not yet been materialized, come into existence.

What are you hoping for? What do you see materializing in your life and in those lives of the ones you love?

_____

_____

_____

And it shall come to pass in the last days, saith God, I will pour out My Spirit upon all flesh: and your sons and your daughters shall prophesy, and your young men shall see visions, and your old men shall dream dreams. Acts 2:17

The Holy Spirit is available to all right now. Ask Him to come into your life and ask for His Divine knowledge to be made known to you, right now, right in your life as it is currently. Ask Him to tell you what important information you need to operate in today's world. Education is great, but the wisdom that the Holy Spirit can give you will trump any earned degree, any time! Let the Holy Spirit tell you when you should do certain things. Put paper and pencil next to your bed and tell the Holy Spirit in your prayers before bed, you wish Him to tell you things in your dreams that will help you in your life tomorrow. Tell Him what you hope to take place in your life now. Tell Him, OUT LOUD, that you will write down His instructions when you wake up, and then Do IT! You will be wonderfully surprised when you read what instructions you have written down! I have written things down, gone to work without reading them, came home from work and read them: and WOW, was so surprised!

The Holy Spirit should always be consulted before you make any decision. Ask Him if you should take this job? Or should you buy this house, or should you marry this person? He'll tell you. ASK.

And I say unto you, Ask, and it shall be given you; seek, and you shall find; knock, and it shall be opened unto you. Luke 11:9

Sometimes I ask God for certain things in my life and I don't receive what I asked for. Or I receive something different, entirely. Why is this so if God promised to hear my prayers and answer my requests? I believe that we are at all different levels of our faith journey. Some as toddlers, or young children, some older teens and young adults, etc.. Why would God give me a million dollars if I wasn't ready to do HIS good works with that money? Why would He give me an empire, when I have a hard time running my own life? Start with the small things in life and Ask God to bring things into your life as You grow and as You become worthy and capable of handling more. It doesn't mean you won't receive them into your life, ever, it means there is more learning and faith building on your part before it can work for you.

For you say, I am rich; I have prospered and grown wealthy, and I am in need of nothing, and you do not realize and understand that you are wretched, pitiable, poor, blind, and naked. Revelations 3:17

Why would this be? If I am rich, why would people consider me pitiable and wretched? Why don't we have any problem with actors, famous singers, CEO's and polititians being rich? Why don't we give it a thought that some people are millionaires and billionaires? How come it's ok for these men and women who have no relationship with God to become wealthy in money and things and we suffer and lack all the time?

Because People of God would do things differently with the money and wealth they obtain than people that are of this world, the people the devil encourages. Evil dwells alongside us all the time. God's Last Will and Testament is our guide to understanding how to opperate in this world, during this time, and how to prosper! God teaches us how to turn away from evil and to follow Jesus. God gives us the words we need to fight the devil and the spirits of evil. Evil is a spirit. Evil is the opposite of Faith. Faith in what God says will make the devil flee away from us. The devil does everything he can to make you believe that what God says He will do in the Bible for your lives won't happen. He tries to convince you that there is no God and that people that follow God are foolish and weak. He tells you everything to be afraid of so you won't believe God will protect you and build you up and prosper you.

When evil comes, you fight with the Word of God. When you hear you are worthless? You declare that you are the Blessed child of God! You shout that Jesus died for your sins and His Blood cleansed your soul and has promised that He would not leave you nor forsake you! You fight every evil thought with the Word of God. You cast it down and say I will not accept that thought! Jesus says I am the Righteousness of God. I am Saved, I am Blessed, I am always in the Forefront of His Mind! You cast down that fear and doubt with the Words of Faith! Don't let that evil spirit have at you! God created the spirits that haunt, He is greater than all of them! They only have as much power as YOU give them. Don't give them any power. You are the child of the Most High God Almighty! You have no reason to fear.

What kinds of things have people said about you?
What things tore you down, made you feel inferior?
Do you feel foolish about your wanting to be a part of
the family of God?

_____

_____

_____

Now that I believe, and I profess with my mouth that I believe Jesus is Lord, that I plead His shed blood over my life and the lives of those I love and pray for daily, how should I speak as a covenant person?

The thief (the devil) comes to steal, to kill and destroy. I am come that they may have and enjoy life, and to have it in abundance, till it overflows. John 10:10

You tell that evil devil that now you know you are a Blessed Child of God. You tell him that he can try to tear you down all he wants, but Your God lifts you up and sets you on a high place. He Wills to prosper me. He Wills to make me whole and healthy. He Wills to listen to my hopes and dreams and to ANSWER my prayers. He Wills to protect me and give me a long and wonderful life until I say it is enough and then to enter into my eternal home with Him. You tell him that you have planted seeds that God Wills to have you harvest. You tell him that you can be trusted and that you do all God has told you to do. You tell him that the Holy Spirit is there helping you minute by minute and that you are never alone.

The Lord will be my refuge and my high tower in times of oppression, and a stronghold in times of trouble.

Psalms 9:9

The Lord is my light and my salvation; whom shall I fear? The Lord is the stronghold of my life; of whom shall I be afraid? Psalms 27:1

When you fall, get a Bible out and read it. When you stumble over a troubling problem, get out that Bible, again. It is not a place to keep important papers, or hide money. It is a map to the hidden riches of life and a manual in how to opperate and overcome problems in this life. You are not alone. You have a LOVE LETTER from God Almighty to learn from and to turn to everyday. You have a brother named Jesus. You have a Holy Helper, the Holy Spirit. And you have a God who loves you and knows you, even with all of your faults! He only asks you to Trust Him, to lean on Him.

Though I speak with the tongues of men and of angels, and have not love, I am becoming a noisy gong or a clanging cymbal. And if I have the gift of prophecy, and understand all mysteries, and all knowledge; and though I have all faith, so that I could remove mountains, and have not love, I am nothing. And though I give all my goods to feed the poor, and though I give my body to be burned, and not have love, it profits no one. Love is patient, love is kind, love is never envious or boils over with jealousy, love is not boastful, and does not put itself on display.... Love never fails..... And now abide in faith, hope and love, and the greatest of these three is love. I Corinthians 12:1-13

Be holy as God is Holy. Strive to do right. Give. Forgive. Obey God's commandments. Go to Church and Sow at least 10% into God's kingdom. Remember, it's not to the church, or the minister/priest that we are sowing money to.... it's to do God's work and to make the necessary exchange for God to release the Blessings into your life. Jesus exchanged himself for our sinful lives, and we honor God by exchanging some of our dimes on a dollar for all that He has done for us and for us to show God how much we love and honor Him. Set today's date. See what this next year has in store for you! And God Wills to Bless You! Get yourself in line to be in the Will!

<u>You Want to be in This Will! AMEN!</u>

Today's date is

_____

God Bless!

I would love to thank My Lord and Savior, Jesus the Blessed Christ, that has and continues to Bless my life, my family and community. I am eternally grateful for all the help I have had from the beginning of my existance. I do as I preach and contiune to volunteer my time to my community. I am a tither and tithe at least 10% of everything I earn. I dream big and I expect my harvest to explode onto the scene that I live in everyday. I would like to express thanks to those who have mentored me, My husband and Son, my mom and sisters, M. Johnson, S.Townsend, J. Craigmile, J. Welch, K. Avery, D.Day. My church community, Joyce Meyers, Bill and Gloria Gaither, Creflo Dollar, Billy Graham, Oral Roberts, Kenneth and Gloria Copeland, The Women of Faith Conventions.

Cynthia Saarie is the owner of Forevermore. She is the wife of Arthur (Skip) Saarie and they reside in Phoenix, NY. They have a son, Neal and his wife, Holly, that live nearby. Cynthia has sung for over 35 years for any Veteran's organization that has asked, for many civic functions, weddings, funerals, the Pennellville, NY Christmas Cantata, the Phoenix Community Band and of course, for her church, the First United Methodist Church of Phoenix. She is a Voice Over Artist recording commercials and narrative commissions, and sings jingles for commercials as well as recording the audio book for this book. Cynthia is a certified Lay Servant Speaker for the United Methodist Church and a member of the National Association of Professional Women. Cynthia would love to come sing or speak for your organization or special occasion. You can reach her through her web site, www.forevermoreonline.com. Logo design by artist, Neal W. Saarie.